King Fox

by Tom Bradman

illustrated by Galia Bernstein

CAMBRIDGE UNIVERSITY PRESS

UCL Institute of Education

Fox woke up late. He was hungry. He stretched and yawned and thought about the delicious fruit and nuts he could have for breakfast.

'What a lovely day,' he said to himself.

Still sleepy, Fox went to find something to eat. After looking for a while, he saw the squirrels hiding in some high branches.

'Hello,' he called up to them, with his sweetest grin. 'Have you got any nuts for my breakfast?'

'Ssshhh! We're hiding,' one whispered back.
'Someone saw Tiger! You have to be quiet!'

But Fox felt too hungry to be quiet and wait,
so he carried on to find someone else.

Fox went to the mice next, then the deer, and even the snakes, but no one wanted to help him find his breakfast. His stomach rumbled loudly.

'I'm so hungry,' he said, rubbing his stomach. 'I must find something to eat soon. Can today get any worse?'

A huge growl answered his question. Tiger was standing just behind him.

'Oh-oh ...'

Before he could think 'huge, terrifying cat',
Fox was running away.

What a terrible day! All Fox wanted was
his breakfast, and now he was going to be
someone else's breakfast.

Tiger was very fast. Fox looked behind him and all he could see was teeth. He dashed onto a forest track, right in front of a cart.

Just in time, Fox leapt out of the way, into a bush.
Shivering with fear, he looked around. Tiger had
vanished, but Fox was too scared to move.

The cart stopped, too. The driver had seen some foresters sitting on the track. He jumped out of the cart and started shouting.

'What are you doing?' he yelled.
'Move out of the way!'

'Yes, master,' they answered.

The men stood up and moved to the side of the track. They kept looking at the back of the cart where a man in yellow was watching them. They looked very frightened.

'They aren't scared of the angry man,' thought Fox. 'They are afraid of the man in the cart. Hmmm, I wonder ...'

After the cart and the men had left, Fox jumped
out of the bush. He looked around, just in case
Tiger was there. He stood as tall as he could,
smoothed down his fur, and took a deep breath.

14

'Now you have a plan,' he muttered to himself.

'You can do this,' he said, in a louder voice.

Then he went looking for Tiger.

It didn't take long to find him. Tiger was circling a tree, growling at the squirrels.

'Come down here,' he demanded. 'I'm hungry.'

'No way!' they cried.

Fox was very scared, but he knew he had to follow his plan.

'What are you doing?' he bellowed in his deepest voice. 'I am King Fox and this is my forest!'

'King of the Forest?' snarled Tiger, prowling towards him. 'You don't look like a king.'

'I'm in charge,' replied Fox, even though he was frightened. 'And eating animals is not allowed.'

'You don't look big enough,' Tiger sneered.

'I'll prove it,' said Fox. 'Squirrels, I am hungry. Give me my breakfast. We will leave as soon as we have eaten.'

'Of course, King Fox,' the squirrels called back, and started throwing down nuts.

'Scaring squirrels doesn't prove anything,' mumbled Tiger, with his mouth full of nuts.

'Follow me,' Fox ordered, eating as he walked.

They went to see the mice, the deer, and
the snakes. Everyone gave some food to make
them go away. They were terrified of Tiger.

'You really *are* in charge round here, aren't you?' said Tiger. 'I haven't eaten this well in years. Thank you, Sir.'

'Just call me King Fox,' he said.

Tiger stalked off in to the forest, and Fox patted his stomach happily. He was finally full.

What a lovely day after all!

King Fox ✿ Tom Bradman

Reading notes written by Sue Bodman and Glen Franklin

Using this book

Developing reading comprehension

This story offers opportunity for inference beyond the text. There are complicated layers of meaning and the book offers a high level of challenge to support comprehension.

Grammar and sentence structure

- The use of dialogue and adverbial phrases serve to indicate how Fox might be saying one thing whilst thinking another. This is an important literary grammar technique which supports comprehension (see page18).

- The choice of verbs illustrates characterisation (for example, when Fox orders Tiger to follow him, on page 20).

Word meaning and spelling

- There are several naturally occurring uses of the /ow/ grapheme. The text provides opportunity to support effective blending through a word to read unfamiliar words and to explore alternative vowel diagraph choices.

- In the guided reading lesson, children can explore new words and effective word choice, and consider how this helps to convey the meaning of the story (e.g. 'bellowed', 'snarled', 'terrified').

Curriculum links

Citizenship – There is potential to relate to children's own experiences of respect and authority, and the text can support discussions about leadership and courage.

Learning Outcomes

Children can:

- discuss story setting and compare with similar traditional tales

- draw together ideas and information from across a whole text

- identify and describe characters

- solve most unfamiliar words on-the-run by blending.

A guided reading lesson

Book Introduction

Give each child a book and read the title to them. Ask them to predict the type of story they are about to read based on the title and illustration. Where does the story take place? Read the back cover blurb together: does this confirm what they were expecting?

Orientation

Recall other stories the children have read where one person or animal has tricked another. In this story, Fox is frightened of Tiger but uses his cunning to outwit him. Say: *This story is about a clever fox. He is hungry but all the animals are so frightened of Tiger that they tell Fox to be quiet and go away. Then something happens that gives Fox an idea. Let's see what happens ...*

Preparation

Page 5: *Fox is looking for food, but the squirrels tell him to be quiet. Why?* Establish that they are frightened of Tiger and look at page 6 together to see how the other animals responded. Tiger appears on page 7!

Now with your partner, look through the book up to page 16, and talk about what happens in the next part of the story. Bring the group back together and ask them to discuss what happened to Fox in the forest. Go to page 13 and ask: 'Why did Fox say: 'Hmmm, I wonder ...'?

Page 16: Use the word *'growling'* to demonstrate reading through a word and identifying known chunks (the /ow/ phoneme